STOP TALKING.
CUT THE CHECK.

Duane O. King, Esq.

ISBN: 978-1-7353827-2-2

I said that I wanted to be a lawyer at a very young age, the road to becoming a successful lawyer has been an arduous journey, each victory (and defeat) has made me a stronger person. I dedicate this book to those who have helped me along the way, from the court clerk that made me refile a document several times, to the much more experienced attorneys who gave me bits of advice to perfect my craft. It has all helped to mold me into the man and lawyer that I am today. Thank You.

CONTENTS

Foreword

I have more than 17 years of experience assisting thousands of clients, many of them repeat clients, who have been injured in motor vehicle collisions. I am licensed to practice law in Washington, DC; Maryland and New York. No two accidents are the same, and neither are the injuries that have been sustained as a result.

In this book, I will draw upon my experience to detail what happens when you get injured in an auto collision. The purpose of this book is to shed light on some things that you may encounter along the way, thank you for taking the time to read it.

Nothing in this book should be taken as, or relied on as legal advice. If you have been injured in an accident, seek the advice of an attorney as soon as possible.

CHAPTER ONE

The First Ten Steps

I was in a car accident. What should I do?

If you have been in a car accident, more than likely, you will be shaken up in the aftermath. You may be confused or disoriented, so take a moment to gather yourself. There are a few things that you should do immediately to ensure your health and safety are protected.

What you do immediately after an accident can mean the difference between a full recovery and a partial recovery, both in terms of your physical health and your monetary compensation. This can be a confusing time, but a critical one nonetheless. Taking the following 10 steps can dramatically help improve your chances of recovering your physical and financial life.

1. **Assess Injuries**. If possible, do not move anyone in the car unless there is an immediate danger to your lives. If you are not injured or have minor injuries, and it is safe to do so, check the other vehicle (if applicable) to assess other involved persons for injuries.

2. **Assess for Additional Danger**. If your vehicle is in a busy intersection or freeway, if you can move the vehicle out of the way of traffic, do so. If you smell gasoline, it may be necessary to move away from the vehicle. If you are alone, in a remote location, and if the collision occurred at night, it is probably best not to exit your vehicle unless there is an immediate risk of additional injury.

3. **Call 911**. Provide your location and details of any injuries. Answer

questions to the best of your ability.

4. **Avoid Confrontation with Other Driver or Passengers**. If you are in a minor accident, you should ask the other driver for their license number and insurance information. Do not apologize and do not assign blame. Anything you say may be used against you later in the process.

5. **Take Pictures and Video of the Accident Scene**. If you are able, and it is safe to do so, use your phone to take pictures and video of the accident scene. If you are unable to, ask a bystander to assist you with this. Pictures and video should be taken of:

- damage to the vehicles
- vehicle license plates
- location of the vehicles
- your injuries
- your passengers' injuries
- a broad view of the accident scene
- any posted signs nearby
- the condition of the roadway

Why is this so important? You should immediately document the scene for two reasons:

A. The location of the vehicles immediately following a collision can be important in determining who was responsible for the accident. Frequently, when trying to prove fault in an accident, it is your version of the accident vs. the version of the other driver. A photograph of the position of the vehicles immediately following the collision is important in making a determination of fault.

B. As much as I would like to believe that most people are honest and ethical, car accidents have served as a stark reminder that this may not be the case. PEOPLE OFTEN FLEE THE SCENE OF A COLLISION, even after they have gotten out of the vehicle to talk to the other driver. I have had several clients who have gotten out and spoken with someone who hit them only to realize seconds later that this person is about to flee the scene of the collision.

Insider Tip: Once you have pictures of the license plate on the other vehicle, your insurance company or attorney can perform a "tag trace" to find the owner of the car and their insurance company. (in the event they give you an expired insurance card).

6. Record Statements. If you speak with the other driver, note whether they admit fault for the accident. You may hear things like:

- "Oh, I didn't see you."
- "It was all my fault."
- "Sorry, I was distracted."

If you are not alone and have passengers, make sure one of your passengers also hears the other driver accept blame for the accident. These types of statements are useful if your case has to go to Court. If the other driver is blaming you for the collision, you should return to your car and wait for the police to arrive.

7. Seek out Witness Statements. If you are able, ask if there are any witnesses around that saw the accident happen. Even if the other driver admitted fault, this does not mean that he will not change his story later when he speaks with the police or his insurance carrier. Regardless of whether the witness stays on the scene to give their account to the police, get the witness contact information.

8. Obtain Medical Assistance. When the police arrive on the scene, they will ask if you are injured. Now is not the time to be a hero. If you are feeling any kind of pain, let the officer know immediately. There is an adrenaline rush that accompanies being involved in a collision. As a result, you may not feel injuries that have occurred, or are developing. If you are unsure as to your injuries, it is fine to tell the officer that "you are not sure" when asked if you are injured. Pain in auto collisions is not always instant. If you say, "I feel fine" or "I am okay" that will become a part of the police accident report. This can be used against you later if you claim injuries at a later time.

9. Go to the Hospital. If you are in obvious pain at the scene, consent to be transported to the hospital by ambulance. Your immediate health is the priority— NOTHING ELSE. Not your vehicle. Not your belongings that are in the car. A police officer may visit the hospital to get your version of what happened.

10. Make a Police Report. After you give your statement, the officer will provide you with your police report number and let you know where your vehicle is stored. Depending on your jurisdiction and the severity of your accident, a police report may not be made. If this is the case, make sure you document as much as possible at the scene since there will be no report made at a later time.

What is Next? Steps to Take in the Days and Weeks Following Your Accident.

Again, the most important thing to think about in the days and weeks following your auto accident is your health and recovery. Second to that is keeping track of any expenses you incur as a result of the accident. This will help ensure that you are made whole financially throughout this process. In the coming days, consider these steps:

1. Continue with medical care.
2. Comply with all doctor orders.
3. Attend all treatments.
4. Start an accident-related health journal to track your symptoms, treatments, and improvement.
5. Start an accident file to keep track of bills, receipts, mileage to and from medical visits, lost income, and other out-of-pocket, accident-related expenses.
6. Contact your car insurance carrier to alert them of the accident - they may be able to help get you money for property damage (more on that in the next chapter).
7. Do not speak with insurance representatives from the other party's insurance carrier without first speaking with a personal injury attorney.

Why do we recommend you do not speak with the other party's insurance?

It's simple—they are not on your side.

They may tell you they are there to help expedite your payments, or that you are required to give a recorded statement. Do not let them bully you! They are specially trained professionals who have no problem denying your claim.

Bottom line - talk to a lawyer first.

CHAPTER TWO

Insurance Coverage

In this chapter, I will discuss what you are entitled to recover after an accident, and how insurance fits into that recovery. I will explain common insurance terms like:

- Collision Coverage
- Comprehensive Coverage
- Liability Coverage
- Uninsured Motorist Coverage
- Underinsured Motorist Coverage
- Umbrella Coverage
- Personal Injury Protection or Medical Payments Coverage

I will also cover some common misconceptions about insurance coverage, so you have all of the relevant information you need to make informed decisions moving forward.

Finally, I will provide some answers to frequently asked questions I get when it comes to auto accidents and insurance coverage.

Types of Insurance Coverage

Collision Coverage

Collision coverage repays you in the event your vehicle collides with another vehicle or fixed object, like an embankment, a tree, or light pole. If you own your vehicle outright, collision coverage is not required. However, if you are leasing or financing a vehicle, collision coverage is required.

Collision coverage does not cover:

- Damage to your car due to natural causes, like hail or falling trees
- Theft of your vehicle
- Damage to another person's vehicle
- Medical bills due to injuries

There are two numbers you want to be familiar with when it comes to any insurance coverage: **Deductibles and Coverage Limits**.

Your deductible is the amount you must pay before your insurance coverage kicks in. For example, you may have a $500 deductible, which means if you have $1,500 in damages to your car, you must pay $500 and your insurance company pays the remaining $1,000.

Coverage limits refer to the total amount your insurance carrier will pay in the event of an accident. Your collision coverage limit is generally the cash value of your car, minus depreciation. So, if you get into an accident in your 2000 Honda Accord and total your vehicle, the insurance company will look at the value of your Honda and pay you for the stated value, minus your deductible.

Comprehensive Coverage

Comprehensive coverage will pay for damage to your vehicle caused by covered events such as theft, vandalism or hail (which are not collision related and are not covered by collision coverage).

Liability Coverage

Liability coverage pays others when you cause an accident. Auto liability coverage is required in most states and covers personal injury and property damage to others if you cause an accident.

Uninsured Motorist Coverage

Uninsured motorist coverage covers you when you are hit by a driver who has no insurance. Since you are unable to make a claim against the uninsured driver, you make a claim with your insurance company.

Your insurance company will cover your personal injury expenses and property damage, up to your coverage limits.

Underinsured Motorist Coverage

Underinsured motorist coverage applies to a case when an at-fault driver does not have sufficient coverage to handle the damage that they have caused. Once you have exhausted the policy limits of the at-fault carrier, you make a claim with your insurance company so that your insurance company can pay you the remaining amount owed.

Umbrella Coverage

Umbrella insurance coverage is an additional policy that covers expenses above and beyond those covered by your traditional insurance coverage. You can obtain umbrella insurance coverage to help pay for medical expenses and property damage caused while driving. Umbrella coverage may also cover situations that are not covered by your existing insurance policies.

You can obtain umbrella coverage to cover things like:

- other people's medical bills for bodily injury for an accident that is your fault
- other people's property damage caused by an accident that is your fault

Note, you cannot obtain umbrella coverage to pay for damages resulting from an accident you have already caused. Umbrella insurance must be purchased prior to an accident.

Personal Injury Protection or Medical Payments Coverage

Personal Injury Protection or Medical Payments Coverage pay when you are injured in an accident. It does not matter if you were the person at fault for the accident, or if another person was at fault. You are entitled to have a portion of your medical bills covered, and in the case of Personal Injury Protection, a portion of your lost wages as well.

Personal Injuries and Insurance Coverage

When you are injured in a car accident and someone else is at fault, you may be eligible to receive compensation for things like:

- **Pain and Suffering** - you may be able to receive money for physical and emotion pain that you have suffered as a result of the accident.
- **Medical Expenses** - the at-fault party is responsible for any medical expenses that you incurred as a result of the accident, including ambulance fees and emergency room treatments, doctors' visits, and physical therapy. You can also be compensated for travel costs associated with appointments, so keep track of your mileage.
- **Lost Wages** - you can recover money for days you missed work; however, it is important to have a disability slip from a doctor that advised you to stay off of work.

Property Damage and Insurance Coverage

Following an accident, your vehicle may be partially or totally inoperable. For most people, this is a pretty serious problem. Our vehicles get us to and from work. They get our kids to school and medical appointments. We rely on our vehicles on a daily basis.

So, what happens when we are without a vehicle?

We rely on insurance.

After an accident, if you expect your insurance company to be involved in handling your claim, you should notify them. If you have collision coverage, your insurance company will pay for your vehicle repair or replacement. Once fault is determined, your insurance company will either accept the loss (in the event you are at fault), or go after the other party's insurance company for repayment. This is called "**subrogation**." This is not something you need to be concerned about, but if you see that term come up, that is what it means.

The big question I always get is this: **How Much Can I Expect to Get for my Vehicle?**

Explaining how property damage awards work to clients is one of the most challenging parts of my job. I say this because, in the eyes of the law, a person is only entitled to the **"appraised" or "fair market value"** of the vehicle. This value often ends up being less than what the vehicle is worth to my client.

I have had my own experience with this very issue:

My first encounter with personal injury law occurred when I had just graduated from law school and was awaiting my bar exam results. One evening I was on my way home, and a Toyota 4Runner came out of nowhere from a side street and ran smack into the front drivers' side of my vehicle.

It was a huge impact. My car was immediately disabled. I jumped out to speak with the people that were responsible. It was a man driving and a woman passenger. They also jumped out.

They apologized to me profusely for what had just happened. The man kept saying, "I'm sorry, I didn't see you. I didn't see you!"

I replied, "Okay, I'm going to call the police right now."

He responded, "Okay, okay I'm just going to move my vehicle out of traffic."

I was still shaken up, as it had all happened so fast. Once he got inside the vehicle, I noticed that the female also got back inside with him. Before I knew it, he had started the car, hit the gas, and was high tailing it from the scene of the collision.

I ran as hard as I could to catch him. While I wasn't able to catch up, I was able to get his license plate number. These were the days before camera phones, so the first thing I did when I exited my vehicle was memorize the other car's license plate number.

As a result of the accident, I sustained whiplash injuries. I retained a local personal injury attorney. He was able to do a tag trace on the vehicle that hit me. It turned out that the car was uninsured.

I was driving a hand-me-down vehicle when I was hit, one that my grandmother had driven for many, many years, a Mercury Grand Marquis. It was declared a total loss after the collision. I only had liability insurance on it, since that was the cheapest option. When I found out that the at-fault vehicle was uninsured, I thought, "Damn, I guess I'm just out of luck since they had no insurance!"

Much to my surprise, I was wrong because I previously purchased ***Uninsured Motorist Coverage*** *as part of my policy. Uninsured motorist coverage protects you when you sustain vehicle damage and injuries that are a result of being hit by a hit-and-run driver or an uninsured motorist.*

In this instance, it was both. I was hit by a hit-and -run driver who was also an uninsured driver. So, I bet you're thinking, "Oh great! You had that coverage, and now you were able to get paid for the car!"

Well that is true, I was able to get paid for my car but I think the appraised value ended up being around $2,000.00 or so. I was so confused and upset, here I was minding my own business trying to get home one night and this uninsured driver plows into my vehicle, causes me to sustain whiplash and back injuries, and now MY insurance company is talking about giving me ONLY $2,000 for my car?! This just didn't make sense to me. There's no way I could use this $2,000.00 to buy a new car or even a comparable used car. That money would only serve as a down payment for another car (I had just amassed over $75,000 in law school debt and wasn't trying to add to that number with a vehicle.) That car was worth much more than $2,000.00 to me. But that did not matter in the eyes of the law. I was only entitled to the "fair market value" for my vehicle, and that was a tough pill to swallow.

My experience was not unlike many, many other peoples' when it comes to getting into a car accident. Not only are we physically sideswiped, we are also emotionally and financially sideswiped. This is not a normal state of existence. Naturally, people have questions.

Let me answer some of the most common property damage questions I get from clients who have been involved in car accidents.

I was just involved in a hit-and-run accident, or an accident with an uninsured driver. Is there any way I can have my vehicle paid for if I only have liability insurance?

Answer: Yes, if you have purchased uninsured motorist coverage, your policy should pay for both your injury and the property damage that has resulted from this collision.

I owned my car outright when I was involved in a car accident that totaled my car. I do not want another car payment. Will the other driver's insurance provide me with a similar vehicle?

Answer: No. The at-fault driver's insurance company is not required to provide you with a similar vehicle. They are only required to give you "fair market value" for your vehicle.

My car appraised at $20,000 before the collision. I had extensive repairs done, but now my car is appraised at $15,000. Can I recover the difference?

Answer: You absolutely can recover it. It is called a **Diminution in Value** claim. This means, if your vehicle sustained extensive damage that resulted in extensive repairs (instead of the car being totaled), you are entitled to the value that your vehicle has diminished as a result of the collision.

Once your car has been repaired, you must get a diminished value appraisal and submit that to the insurance company for payment. In the above example, you as the *claimant* would receive $5,000.00 as the diminished value settlement.

I got into an accident. My car is in a tow yard because the other driver's insurance company is still investigating the accident. Can I let the car stay there until they finish the investigation?

Answer: No, you cannot. There are a number of things that can delay an investigation after an accident, and here are a few:

a) **The insured may not be cooperating with their insurance company.** I am sure you know that when you cause an accident, your insurance rates will likely go up as a result. Rather than "face the fire" and come clean to their insurance company, some people would rather not admit fault to their company, and this can cause serious delays in the investigation.

b) **The policy may not have been active at the time.** If you miss your insurance premium payment date by one day, your insurance is late, and it is also inactive. Researching payment history and verifying if there is an active policy can also cause delays in an insurance investigation.

c) **There may be a dispute as to what happened.** As I mentioned earlier, just because someone admits fault at the scene of an accident, this does not mean that they will admit fault when they speak with their insurance company. If there are conflicting accounts as to what happened, this will also cause delays in the investigation.

Regardless of the reason, leaving your car at a tow yard means that fees are accruing. Many tow yards average about $50 a day in storage fees, each day the insurance company investigates your case, that is another day of storage fees that have accrued.

The law requires a claimant to **mitigate their damages** after an accident. This means that if the insurance investigation is pending, you must take reasonable steps to get your vehicle removed from the tow yard. Yes, yes, I know this accident was not your fault, and you should not be required to come "out of pocket."

I always recommend that my clients use their collision policy to: either get their vehicle fixed, or get paid the cash value if it is declared a total loss. That way, they do not have to worry about waiting on the adverse driver's carrier accepting liability. Yes, you will have to pay your deductible. However, you will be fully reimbursed from either your insurance company once they have been repaid, or by the adverse driver's carrier once responsibility has been accepted.

<u>What type of rental vehicle am I entitled to receive after an accident?</u>

Answer: You are entitled to rent a vehicle similar to the vehicle that was damaged until your car is either fixed, or until you have been paid for your total loss. For example, if you were driving a pickup truck at the time of your accident, you are entitled to a rental pickup truck for the duration of the repairs to your vehicle.

<u>If my car is totaled, can I keep the rental car until I'm able to buy a new car?</u>

Answer: If your vehicle has been declared a total loss, the insurance company will issue you a check for your vehicle. Typically, your rental will be good for a few days after the check has been issued. If at that time you have not gotten a new vehicle you will be responsible for the subsequent rental vehicle charges.

How long am I entitled to keep the rental vehicle?

Answer: If your car is repairable and you pursue a claim through the adverse driver's insurance, you can keep the rental for the amount of time that it takes to fix your car. If you go through your own carrier (because you've decided you do not want to wait to see what the other carrier will do), it will depend on the terms of your policy. For example, if your policy states that your insurance will cover up to $900.00 in rental car expenses, once that $900.00 is exhausted you must return the rental, or pay for it yourself, not withstanding if your car has been fixed or not.

If your vehicle has been declared a total loss, the insurance company will issue you a check for your vehicle, and your rental will be good for a few days after that check has been issued.

The insurance company paid me less for my car than what I owe on the loan. Can they do that?

Answer: Yes, they can. You are entitled to the **fair market value** of your vehicle, not the value that is remaining on your loan. For example, if you owe a $10,000.00 balance on your vehicle, but the appraised value of your vehicle is $8,000.00, the insurance company will issue you a check for $8,000.00. This will leave you with a $2,000.00 balance on your loan unless you have what is called **GAP Insurance**.

Gap insurance provides you protection when you owe more than what the car is worth. If you do not have gap insurance, you will be responsible for the remaining amount on the loan. I have had clients in this predicament and it is literally like adding insult to injury. The client was injured, car was totaled, now they have to heal from their injuries, get a new car, and still pay for the car that they no longer have.

This is not a good situation to be in; however, I always ask clients to look on the bright side, "Well it is good that you're still here. The accident could have been much worse."

What if the person that caused the accident does not have enough

<u>coverage to repair or replace my vehicle?</u>

Answer: Each state has "minimum" insurance coverage requirements. This means that in order to get insurance coverage on your vehicle, it must be "minimally" insured for a certain amount. This can cause problems when an individual does not have enough coverage to pay for a vehicle that they damage.

Example: Sally and John are in an automobile collision. John was deemed to be at fault and he had the minimum coverage on his vehicle which will pay up to $15,000.00 in property damage in an accident. Sally was driving a Porsche 911, valued at $75,000, and her car was declared a total loss as a result of the accident. After John's insurance pays Sally $15,000.00, who is responsible for the other $60,000.00 that's owed on Sally's vehicle? The answer: John is personally responsible for the remaining $60,000.00 to be paid to Sally for her vehicle. Now most people do not have an extra $60,000.00 laying around to pay someone after an accident, so here are Sally's options:

A. **<u>Sue John personally for the amount owed.</u>** It may have been an accident by John (instead of an intentional act), but he still owes Sally for what he did. If he does not have the money to pay Sally for her beautiful Porsche that he totaled, Sally has the option of suing him and getting a judgment against him in a Court of Law for $60,000.00. Once Sally obtains that judgment against John, a lien can be placed on any assets that John has, his wages could be garnished, as well as a host of other things. However, if John does not have the money, he just does not have the money. Sally may be better off choosing another option that is available to her.

B. **<u>Use her own insurance to cover the cost of her vehicle.</u>** When Sally bought her Porsche, she was fully aware of the possibility of someone hitting her vehicle who did not have enough insurance to cover her. When selecting her insurance, she was sure to get "full coverage" that would protect her whether she caused an accident, or she got into an accident and it was someone else's fault. Low and behold she gets into an accident with John who does not have enough coverage. Sally invokes her collision coverage to pay her the fair market value of her vehicle, the only thing Sue has to pay in this instance is her deductible (which will be subtracted from the total loss amount of her vehicle). Sally's insurance carrier would have the option of pursuing John personally for what they paid on Sally's vehicle.

I paid my deductible to my insurance company to get my car fixed. When will I be reimbursed for my deductible?

Answer: When you make the decision to go through your own carrier to fix your vehicle, or pay for your vehicle if it has been declared a total loss, you must pay a deductible at the time your car has been repaired, or have your deductible subtracted from your total loss amount. If the adverse driver's carrier has accepted liability (fault) for the accident, the adverse driver's insurance carrier will reimburse your insurance carrier for what your carrier has paid on your behalf. This will include monies paid to fix or total your vehicle, and also any money paid on your behalf for a rental vehicle.

Can I get my car repaired at the shop of my choice?

Answer: Yes, you can. However, there is a catch to it. When you get into an accident, if your car is still drivable, the insurance company may ask you to have your car appraised at the insurance carrier's approved shop to get an estimate. Once you get that estimate you will have the option of getting it repaired at the carrier's approved shop, or taking the estimate that was prepared to another shop to fix your car.

Oftentimes, the estimate that is prepared at one shop may be more expensive to fix than at another shop. If this happens, the shop where you choose to take your car will issue a "**supplement**" to the insurance company who will have their representative inspect your car, and the insurance company will then issue a check for the additional amount.

As an incentive to getting the car fixed at their shop, insurance companies will sometimes say, "If you get your car fixed here, these repairs are guaranteed for the life of the car." However, if you choose your own shop, you likely will not get that type of warranty on repairs.

In the next chapter, I will talk about your recovery and how best to heal during this time while still ensuring your rights are protected.

CHAPTER THREE
Recovery and Healing

In the last chapter, I discussed various insurance coverages that might apply to a car accident case. However, before you consider settling an accident claim, you need to focus on recovering from the physical injuries caused by the car crash.

Let us take a closer look at the recovery process after an accident and damages related to your physical injuries. Topics I cover in Chapter Three include:

- How Delays in Medical Treatment Can Hurt Your Car Accident Claim
- Proving the Car Accident Caused Your Injuries
- Importance of Completing Medical Treatment Before Settling an Insurance Claim
- Injury Damages Claimed In a Car Accident

How Delays in Medical Treatment Can Hurt Your Car Accident Claim

If you sustained serious injuries from the car accident, you likely were transported to the emergency room by EMS directly from the accident scene. It is generally best to go directly to the hospital after a car accident to be checked by a medical professional.

It can be difficult to know if you were injured in a car accident for several reasons. The shock of being involved in a crash can often mask symptoms of injuries. Some injuries may not present symptoms for several hours or days following an accident. It is wise to have a complete physical following an accident to protect your health and your legal rights.

Common Accident Injuries

Car crashes can cause a variety of injuries. Some injuries may heal with time and rest. Other injuries may require moderate medical intervention, such as medications and physical therapy. Traumatic and life-threatening injuries can require surgery and months of recovery. In some cases, an accident victim may never recover fully from the injuries sustained in a traffic accident.

Common car accident injuries include:

- Head and brain injuries, including concussions, traumatic brain injury (TBI), skull fractures, and hematomas
- Neck and shoulder injuries, including whiplash and rotator cuff tears
- Back and spinal cord injuries, including ruptured discs, fractures, and paralysis
- Bone fractures and broken bones
- Soft tissue injuries to the ligaments, tendons, and muscles
- Lacerations and puncture wounds
- Facial trauma, hand injuries, knee injuries, and ankle injuries
- Internal bleeding and damage to internal organs
- Scarring and disfigurement

Can I Receive Compensation if I Did Not See a Doctor After a Car Accident?

Yes, you can recover money for an accident claim if you did not immediately seek medical treatment for injuries. However, it can be more difficult to prove that your injuries resulted from the car crash.

To recover money for injuries sustained in a car accident, you must prove that the collision was the "**direct and proximate**" cause of your injuries. In other words, your injuries would not have occurred had it not been for the car accident.

Delays in medical care give the insurance company for the other driver a reason to argue that the accident did not cause your injuries. The insurance company may argue that if you had been injured in the car crash, you would have seen a doctor immediately following the accident. The company may argue that your injuries occurred because of another event in the weeks following the accident.

INSIDER TIP: Never tell a police officer or emergency medical services that you do not think you are injured after an accident. If you do not want to go to the hospital by ambulance, or you don't think it is necessary, it is better to say that you are going to see your family physician for an examination to determine your injuries instead of saying you do not think you are hurt or you do not think your injuries are severe.

Insurance Companies Try to Limit Liability for Claims

An insurance company will try to limit its liability for an injury claim. It is best not to give the insurance company any reason to deny or undervalue your injury claim. Seeking immediate medical care after a car accident is one of the best ways to prove that the car accident caused your injuries.

Proving the Car Accident Caused Your Injuries

Most states are fault-based states for car accident claims. You must prove that another driver or party was responsible for the cause of the crash to recover compensation from that driver for your injuries and damages.

A few states have no-fault insurance laws that require drivers to file claims through their insurance carrier after an accident. Accident victims are only permitted to file claims or lawsuits against other drivers if they meet certain criteria, such as sustaining catastrophic injuries or substantial financial damages.

Seek Immediate Medical Attention After a Car Accident to

Document Your Injuries

You must prove that your injuries were caused by the car accident to recover money from an insurance company. Medical evidence is the best way to prove that the collision caused your injuries. As discussed above, immediate medical attention is best. If you did not go to the hospital after the accident, see your physician as soon as possible for a complete examination.

When you see a physician for a car accident injury, make sure that you tell the doctor you were involved in a car crash. The doctor's notes from your visit will be a part of your claim. Therefore, you want to make sure that your doctor is aware that the reason you are seeking treatment is that you were involved in a car crash.

Some Injuries Are More Difficult to Diagnose

Give a detailed accounting of all symptoms, so the symptoms are documented in the medical records. Even if it is just occasionally that you experience numbness or tingling in your shoulders and arms, make sure that you report these symptoms to your physician.

Any symptom, regardless of how minor or how frequent, could be an indication of a serious injury. Your doctor needs to know about every symptom to diagnose your injuries correctly after an accident.

Your physician may need to perform numerous diagnostic tests to determine the exact cause of your symptoms. The results of these tests can be used to prove that your injuries resulted from the car accident.

Your physician may recommend X-rays, CT scans, an MRI, blood tests, and other diagnostic tests.

Examples of medical evidence that can be used to prove the car crash caused your injuries include:

- Your patient chart
- Physician and nurse's notes in your chart
- Medical reports from emergency medical services and EMTs at

the accident scene

- Emergency room reports
- Surgical notes and reports
- Results from diagnostic tests and laboratory tests
- Records and notes from occupational therapists, vocational therapists, and physical therapists
- Testimony from medical experts

It can be overwhelming to go through multiple diagnostic tests or meet with specialists and numerous medical providers. However, it may be necessary to diagnose your injury correctly so that you can receive the treatment you need to recover from an automobile accident. These tests also provide the documentation and evidence necessary to prove that the accident caused your injuries.

Important Do's & Don'ts to Remember

- **DON'T** make statements after the car accident, such as, "I'm fine" or "I'm okay." Don't say, "I don't think I am hurt," or "My injuries are not that severe."
- **DON'T** decline being transported to the hospital if EMS personnel recommend going to the emergency room.
- **DON'T** run to the other vehicle to check on the passengers. Be cautious of your actions immediately after the accident. If possible and safe to do so, limit movement until EMS arrives.
- **DO** tell EMS personnel all of your symptoms. Don't exaggerate, but also do not play the hero.
- **DO** seek immediate medical attention after a car accident.
- **DON'T** return to work before your doctor releases you to do so. Returning to work or normal daily activities sooner than recommended gives the insurance company another reason to argue your injuries were not as serious as you now claim.
- **DO** complete the entire medical treatment plan prescribed by

your physician. Keep all follow-up appointments with your physicians and complete physical therapy, occupational therapy, or other recommended treatments.

- **DO** limit your activities. Going on vacation, participating in recreational activities, volunteering, packing to move, and other actions require physical effort. It is difficult to claim that you could not work if you can continue engaging in other activities that require physical effort.
- **DON'T** use social media or allow others to post photos or information about your activities online during your claim. The insurance company may obtain that information to use against you when settling your claim or going to trial. Some courts have granted access to private accounts for use in court proceedings.

Sadly, it is up to the accident victim to prove that a negligent driver caused the victim's injuries. Seeing a doctor as soon as possible and following the treatment plan helps you protect your legal right to receive fair compensation for your accident injuries.

Importance of Completing Medical Treatment Before Settling an Insurance Claim

Completing medical treatment is important for your health. Your best chance of recovering fully from an automobile accident is to work closely with your physicians to complete the course of medical treatment.

However, it is also important that you complete medical treatment before you settle an insurance claim. Settling an insurance claim **before** you complete medical treatment could result in the loss of thousands of dollars in compensation.

WARNING! ***The insurance company may pressure you to settle early.***

If an insurance company recognizes that you were injured, it may attempt to settle your claim before you complete your treatment. The reason is simple. If you settle your claim before you realize the severity of your injuries and damages, the insurance company can save money.

Settling your claim means you cannot receive any more money for your claim. After you settle a claim and sign a release, you cannot sue for additional money. Therefore, you are responsible for the cost of any further medical treatment. You also cannot receive reimbursement for any other financial losses after you settle the injury claim.

It is never advisable to settle a personal injury claim, or an insurance claim before your doctor releases you from treatment. There is no way to know whether you will sustain permanent disabilities or impairments until you complete the treatment plan prescribed by your physician.

Permanent Impairments and Disabilities Caused by Accidents

Your doctor will advise you when you reach **Maximum Medical Improvement** (MMI). For some accident victims, MMI means that they recovered completely from their accident injuries and can return to normal activities of daily living.

However, for some accident victims, MMI means that they have reached the point in their treatment at which no further medical treatment will help them reach full recovery. In other words, they sustained a permanent impairment or disability because of the auto accident.

If you reach MMI without full recovery, your doctor issues a prognosis. The prognosis typically explains the impairment or disability and may include a percentage of impairment. For example, someone who is completely paralyzed may be 100 percent impaired. On the other hand, someone who loses partial use of their arm may experience a 20 percent impairment.

Accident victims who sustain permanent impairments or disabilities may be entitled to additional compensation. They may receive compensation for the loss of use of a body part or other impairment. They may also receive compensation for future medical costs and loss of income.

In many cases, your attorney retains medical experts and financial experts to assist in estimating the cost of future damages for disabilities and impairments. Experts provide crucial testimony regarding how your life will be impacted by the impairment, including financial losses and loss of quality of life.

The testimony from experts helps establish the value of injury damages caused by a car accident.

Injury Damages Claimed In a Car Accident

Physical injuries caused by a car accident can result in a variety of damages. **Damages** are the losses you experience because of the car accident ,including your physical injuries. Damages are typically divided into two categories: **economic damages and noneconomic damages.**

Economic Damages Related to Car Accident Injuries

Economic damages are the financial losses and expenses related to the accident and your injuries. If the other driver or another party is fully responsible for the cause of the accident, you are generally entitled to receive full compensation for all economic damages. There could be some factors that might impact your rights, but if you did not contribute to the cause of the accident, and have proof of your economic damages, you should be entitled to full compensation.

Examples of economic damages associated with an automobile accident include, but are not limited to:

- Medical care and expenses
- Prescriptions, over-the-counter medications, and medical equipment
- Physical therapy, occupational therapy, and vocational therapy
- Counseling and mental health treatment

- Personal care expenses and help with household chores
- Travel expenses
- Loss of income, including diminished earning capacity and loss of future wages and benefits

The amount you receive for economic damages depends on a variety of factors. The best way to ensure that you receive maximum compensation for economic damages is to document your financial losses throughout your case carefully.

Keep copies of all receipts, invoices, statements, and other evidence of expenses and losses incurred because of the accident, your injury, and your recovery.

Noneconomic Damages Related to Car Accident Injuries

Noneconomic damages are much more difficult to prove and document because these damages are unique to the individual. Noneconomic damages are often referred to as "**pain and suffering**" damages because they relate to the physical, emotional, and mental pain and distress caused by the accident and your injuries.

Pain and suffering damages also relate to the permanent injuries, impairments, scarring, disfigurement, and loss of enjoyment or quality of life you experience because of the accident and your injuries. For example, you may experience depression, anxiety, or PTSD because of the accident.

You may be unable to return to normal activities of daily living, such as taking care of your children, participating in hobbies or recreational activities, or socializing with friends and family. For some accident victims, simple tasks like bathing and dressing may be extremely challenging or impossible without assistance.

INSIDER TIP: Keeping a pain and suffering journal can help prove the level of noneconomic damages. In your journal, note your daily pain levels, activities you cannot perform, events you miss, and how the injuries impact your relationships with family and friends.

Describe your state of mind and how your injuries impact your emotional health.

Let us Look at an Example of a Personal Injury Case

Each accident victim's journey to recovery is unique, just as every personal injury case is different. However, looking at some examples can help you understand the injury damages caused by car accidents. It can also help you understand what types of damages you may receive when filing a personal injury claim.

Physical Injuries & Financial Damages

Example: A car accident caused a young woman, Karen, to sustain broken bones in her leg and a traumatic brain injury. She is rushed to the emergency room from the accident scene. She is treated in the emergency room, released, and sent to an orthopedic surgeon. The surgeon recommends surgery. At this point, Karen has incurred expenses related to the ambulance ride, emergency room visit, doctor's bills, surgery costs, and physical therapy after surgery.

However, a couple of weeks after the accident, Karen begins suffering from chronic headaches, unusual fatigue, dizziness, ringing in the ears, and vomiting. Some of the symptoms could be related to the head injury, but she goes back to the doctor.

The doctor refers her to a neurologist who, after conducting a CT scan and MRI, diagnoses a severe traumatic brain injury (TBI). Karen has now incurred additional medical expenses with more to come as she continues to follow her doctor's treatment plan.

During this time, she is unable to work and is losing substantial income because of the accident. She also has to purchase a special bed because her headaches increase in severity when she lays flat. She needs a bed to raise her head and her leg as she recovers. Her doctor estimates it could take six to eight months before she recovers fully from her injuries. Each day, she incurs additional financial losses.

At the completion of her treatment, Karen's doctor tells her that she will likely suffer from chronic headaches from the TBI, and the fractured leg may impair some physical activities and increases her risk of developing arthritis in the future.

To calculate her economic damages, we must gather and include all of her medical expenses. We also must include the cost of necessary at-home medical equipment, the cost of home personal care, assistance with household chores, travel expenses, over-the-counter medications, and loss of income.

The Emotional & Mental Damages Caused by the Accident

As a result of the accident, Karen subsequently becomes severely depressed. She experiences flashbacks of the accident and has anxiety each time she travels in a vehicle. Her quality of life has decreased because she is unable to enjoy the same activities she did before the accident. Her relationship with family and friends has diminished as they continue their lives while she is confined mostly to her home.

Karen enters counseling and therapy to deal with the emotional and mental distress caused by the accident and her injuries. The treatment increases the cost of economic damages (medical bills incurred), but they also help prove pain and suffering, which are the noneconomic damages portion of her claim.

Karen also keeps a journal that details her daily struggles and challenges as she recovers from the accident. She includes details such as not being able to celebrate her 30th wedding anniversary, her granddaughter's first birthday, and not being with her mother when her aunt passed away. She also notes her struggles each day with pain and chronic headaches that severely diminish her relationship with her spouse, family members, and friends.

Karen is devastated that she has scars on her leg from the surgery, and she has a noticeable limp that requires her to use a cane when she needs to go to the grocery store or out to eat. She is anxious about the attention she feels she receives from the disfigurement and the limp.

Even though none of these damages have an invoice or a bill to quantify the value of the damages for a personal injury claim, an experienced attorney working with mental health professionals can explain how these damages impact the victim's life. They can use this evidence to argue for maximum compensation for noneconomic damages.

Seeking Legal Advice for a Car Accident Claim

Calculating damages for a car accident claim can be difficult. Depending on the severity of the injury, an accident victim may be entitled to significant future damages. A personal injury attorney will have experience calculating the value of your damages, and can also help you access experts who can provide crucial evidence to improve your chance of recovering fair and full compensation for your claim.

In the next chapter, I will discuss your medical bills and what can be done following an accident to ensure that you are made whole, which includes making sure that your medical bills are paid in full.

CHAPTER FOUR
Medical Bills

Obtaining prompt medical care after a traffic accident is essential for your health and a personal injury claim. It is best to see a doctor as soon as possible after an accident because insurance companies use delays in medical treatment to deny and undervalue injury claims.

However, it can be difficult to obtain medical care if you do not have medical coverage or health insurance coverage. In this chapter, I discuss some of the challenges faced by car accident victims as they attempt to obtain the medical care they need after an accident injury.

Common Types of Medical Treatment and Care After a Car Accident

Each accident claim is unique. The types and severity of your injuries dictate the type and level of medical treatment you might need after a collision.

Common types of medical treatment included in a traffic accident claim include, but are not limited to:

- EMS treatment and transportation
- Emergency room visits
- Hospitalizations
- Surgeries
- Physicians' bills, including general practice doctors, internists, surgeons, anesthesiologists, radiologists, etc.
- Diagnostic testing includes X-rays, blood work, MRIs, and CT

Scans

- Prescription medications and OTC medications
- Medical supplies and medical equipment
- Various forms of therapy, including physical, occupational, vocational, rehabilitation, counseling, and therapy
- Personal care costs, including assistance with the activities of daily living (ADLs), such as dressing, bathing, feeding, etc.

The cost of medical care after an accident can be expensive. Who pays for these costs? Let us take a closer look at that question.

The Other Driver's Car Insurance Company Does Not Pay Your Medical Bills During Treatment

Even though the other driver may have caused your car accident, the insurance company for the other driver does not pay your medical bills during your treatment. The insurance company may reimburse you for the medical expenses you incurred when your claim is settled.

Until the personal injury claim settles, you are responsible for the payment of your medical bills. In some cases, an accident victim could be stuck with the medical bills from an accident the victim did not cause even after the claim settles.

How Can You Pay for Medical Treatment After a Car Accident?

Because the insurance provider for the at-fault driver will not pay any money until you agree to settle the claim in full, it is up to you to pay for your medical care after a car accident. There are several options for paying for medical treatment after a traffic accident.

Health Insurance Coverage

If you have health insurance coverage, your health insurance provider should pay for medical treatment for injuries sustained in an accident. Health insurance coverage includes benefits provided by private health insurance companies, group employment policies, Medicaid, and Medicare. However, you are responsible for the payment of any co-pays and non-covered costs according to your insurance policy.

Important Note! Your health insurance company, including Medicaid and Medicare, may assert a claim for reimbursement for the money they paid related to the accident injuries. We discuss these claims in more detail later in the chapter under the subrogation section.

Med Pay or Personal Injury Protection

If you have Med Pay or Personal Injury Protection (PIP) insurance on your car insurance policy, you may use these coverages to pay for medical bills after a car accident. Med Pay and PIP are a form of no-fault insurance. Some states require no-fault insurance as their basic car insurance requirements.

Under Med Pay, PIP, or other forms of no-fault insurance, your insurance policy pays your medical bills associated with the car accident regardless of who was at fault for the crash. You do not need to prove that another driver caused the traffic accident to receive benefits under Med Pay or PIP. Even if you caused the accident, or you were partially at fault for causing the accident, you can use PIP and Med Pay to pay for medical care after a crash.

You can receive benefits under PIP and Med Pay immediately, which can be very helpful in ensuring that you receive the medical treatment you need after an automobile accident.

Hospital Liens

Public hospitals are required to treat individuals who require medical care regardless of whether they have insurance. Therefore, if you need surgery or emergency medical care, you can receive that care at the hospital.

However, the hospital has a hospital lien against any proceeds you receive from your personal injury case. Hospital liens must be paid from the proceeds of a personal injury settlement or jury award before the accident victim receives money for other damages.

Medical Lien Agreements

Private physicians are not required to treat you if you are unable to pay for the treatment. However, physicians are familiar with how a personal injury claim works. You must receive treatment and document your injuries before you can recover compensation from the party who caused your car accident.

Therefore, some private medical providers are willing to accept a written agreement promising to pay any outstanding medical bills related to the auto accident from the proceeds you receive for a personal injury claim. The written medical lien agreement is a valid contract between you and the doctor's office.

If you do not receive any money for the car accident claim, you are responsible for the payment of the medical bills secured by the lien. The doctor's office can pursue the debt through various debt collection methods. Medical lien agreements must also be paid from the settlement proceeds for your injury claim before you receive any money for pain and suffering damages or loss of income damages.

Medical liens are not a perfect solution, but they can help accident victims obtain the medical treatment they need while they work on recovering compensation for their car accident claim.

INSIDER TIP! Do not accept fault or admit fault when receiving medical treatment. Do not say you are sorry or wish the accident had not happened. Other than describing your injuries to your medical providers, do not discuss how the crash occurred or give details to the insurance company.

Talk to a car accident lawyer as soon as possible. The things you say during treatment could have a significant impact on your chances of recovering full compensation for your car accident claim.

Subrogation Claims Filed By Health Insurance Providers Reduce Compensation Amounts

Medical treatment liens and hospital liens can lower the amount of money you receive for your pain and suffering or loss of income after a car accident. However, subrogation rights are another legal lien against personal injury proceeds that can impact the amount of money you might receive for a personal injury claim.

When a health insurance company, Medicaid, or Medicare pays medical bills related to an accident injury, those entities have what is called a right to subrogation. A subrogation claim is simply a claim against personal injury proceeds for the amount of money paid for medical treatment related to the injuries that are the subject of the personal injury claim.

For example, a negligent driver caused a crash that resulted in a broken leg. You needed surgery and several weeks of physical therapy. Your employer's health insurance company paid $50,000 in medical bills related to your car accident. When you settle your car accident claim, your health insurance provider is entitled to repayment of the $50,000 from your settlement proceeds.

The reason behind subrogation claims is that a portion of your settlement claim includes the cost of medical care. That portion of the claim should be paid to the medical providers. If a third party paid those bills, the third party is entitled to reimbursement.

Negotiating Medical Lien Claims & Subrogation Claims

Unfortunately, there are many accident cases in which the victim does not receive compensation or all damages for which they are entitle. There may be a problem with the case, or there may be insufficient insurance to pay the claim in full. In those cases, the victim may receive nothing for their pain and suffering and loss of income after payment of subrogation claims and health claims.

Experienced personal injury lawyers negotiate with medical providers, health insurance companies, and other providers to accept a lower amount to satisfy medical liens and subrogation claims. Many providers are willing to work with accident victims who will receive very little to nothing for their pain and suffering and other damages once all medical liens and subrogation claims are paid in full.

Working with an attorney who has experience handling personal injury claims is strongly advised if you sustain serious injuries, which may require substantial medical costs that you cannot afford to pay.

How Can I Be Stuck with Medical Bills for an Accident I Did Not Cause?

No Insurance Coverage

If the party responsible for causing your crash did not have insurance coverage, you may be stuck with the medical bills from an accident you did not cause. You may be able to use health insurance or your car insurance coverage to help pay some of the bills, but uninsured drivers cause thousands of dollars in damages for which they are never forced to pay.

A car accident attorney investigates the at-fault driver to determine if the driver has assets available to pay the debt. However, in most cases, if a person does not have car insurance coverage, the person does not have any assets that can be levied to pay an injury claim.

Attorneys conduct investigations to identify any other parties who may have liability in an uninsured driver claim. Attorneys also determine if a victim carries *underinsured* motorist coverage, or *uninsured* motorist coverage on the victim's car insurance policy. For example, an employer or the owner of the vehicle may have insurance that would cover the collision, or have property that can be levied to pay the claim. Those types of coverages could reimburse the victim for unpaid medical bills when an at-fault driver did not have insurance or insufficient insurance coverage to pay an injury claim in full.

Not Enough Liability Insurance

Most states in the United States use a fault-based theory for payment of damages in a car accident case. The driver who caused the accident is responsible for compensating the victims for losses, including the cost of medical treatment, personal care, and mental health treatment.

However, the state minimum liability insurance amounts vary by state. Some states have very low insurance requirements. The Insurance Information Institute (III) publishes a list of the automobile financial responsibility laws by state on its website.[1]

According to the 2018 III list of insurance responsibility by state, some states require as little as $15,000 in bodily injury recovery. If an accident victim breaks their leg, requires surgery, and needs physical therapy, the medical bills for treatment quickly exceed $15,000. Therefore, the victim could be stuck with any medical bills that exceed $15,000. Furthermore, there would be no money for other damages, such as loss of income, pain, and suffering.

For victims who sustain traumatic injuries or catastrophic injuries, the medical bills could exceed $100,000 or more. If the victim sustains a permanent disability or impairment, ongoing medical and personal care could total hundreds of thousands, or millions of dollars over a lifetime.

---

[1] https://www.iii.org/automobile-financial-responsibility-laws-by-state

Disputed Fault Claims

In cases involving disputed fault, the insurance company blames the accident victim for causing the crash or contributing to the cause of the crash. If the defense strategy is successful, a victim may not receive full compensation for their medical bills and expenses.

For example, the defense attorney claims that you were speeding at the time of the accident. The jury accepts the argument and determines your speed contributed to the cause of the accident by 30 percent. Therefore, the compensation you can receive for your accident is reduced by 30 percent. The reduction in the jury award could leave you with unpaid medical bills.

Also, the insurance company or other defendant may claim that the car accident did not cause your injuries. Delays in medical care are used by insurance companies to raise this defense. If a jury or judge agrees with the defense strategy, you are unable to recover compensation for any medical bills incurred for treatment of injuries not sustained in the car accident.

Never Settle Before You Reach Maximum Medical Recovery

It can be tempting to settle a personal injury claim before completing medical treatment because you need money to pay medical bills or other costs. However, once you settle your personal injury claim, you cannot receive any additional money from the insurance provider or the person who caused your car accident. If you discover that you need additional surgery, or have an injury that you were not aware of, you are limited to the amount you received when you settled the claim.

Maximum Medical Improvement

Maximum Medical Improvement (MMI) is the point at which further medical treatment will not improve your condition. For some accident victims, MMI means a full recovery. However, for other accident victims, MMI includes an impairment rating. The impairment rating refers to the level of disability or impairment that is permanent.

For example, an accident victim who is completely paralyzed probably has a 100 percent impairment rating. An accident victim who sustains a back injury that limits their ability to work or perform some daily activities has an impairment rating based on the severity of the disability.

Why Wait to Reach MMI Before Settling An Injury Case?

Reaching MMI before settling your personal injury claim is crucial. Accident victims are entitled to compensation for permanent disabilities and impairments caused by the auto accident. The compensation for permanent impairments and disabilities may include ongoing medical care, personal care, future loss of income, diminished earning capacity, physical pain, emotional suffering, and diminished quality of life. The amount of compensation related to permanent disabilities could be substantial.

Therefore, do not be tempted by an insurance company offer to settle your claim early in your case. The insurance company may realize that your claim will be significant and it is attempting to avoid substantial liability by paying your injury claim before you understand the full extent of your injuries.

Patience – It Can Be Difficult, But Very Rewarding

It can take a long time to settle a personal injury claim, especially in cases involving traumatic or catastrophic injuries. The length of your treatment is one of the overriding factors that determines how long it will take to complete your claim.

However, if an insurance company is dragging the case out after your doctor states that you have reached MMI, the insurance company may be attempting to allow the **deadline to file** a personal injury lawsuit to pass. An insurance company dragging a case out is an indication you need to talk to a personal injury lawyer immediately.

Also, if your medical treatment will take months or over a year to complete, you may want to talk to a personal injury lawyer now. There are deadlines to file claims after a motor vehicle accident. You do not want to allow those deadlines to expire because you could lose your legal right to pursue a claim. The sooner you begin working with a personal injury lawyer, the faster the lawyer can start protecting your legal right to a fair settlement for injuries sustained in a car accident.

Work With a Personal Injury Lawyer to Document Medical Bills & Damages

In addition to working with an attorney to ensure that the deadline to file a personal injury claim does not expire, or to negotiate subrogation claims, there is another advantage of working with a personal injury lawyer related to medical bills.

Make Sure You Include All Damages in Your Injury Claim

Your personal injury attorney works closely with you to document all expenses related to your accident injuries, treatment, and recovery. Many accident victims are not aware that they may be entitled to other damages related to medical treatment.

For example, if your condition requires that you need safety bars in your shower so that you do not fall, you may be entitled to reimbursement for that cost as a medical expense. Likewise, if you purchase over-the-counter medications and supplies related to your injury, you can include those costs in your car accident claim.

Even Little Known and Overlooked Damages

You may be entitled to compensation if your credit rating significantly decreased because of the unpaid medical bills. If the insurance company acted in bad faith to delay the settlement of your claim, your credit score could suffer because you must wait longer to pay medical providers, who may file collection actions that appear on your credit report. A personal injury attorney can argue that you are entitled to additional financial damages related to a decrease in your credit rating because of the actions of the insurance company.

Working to maximize the claim for medical expenses and related damages is crucial to ensuring that you receive as much as possible for your personal injury claim.

In the next chapter, I discuss loss of income related to an accident claim. Many accident victims sustain substantial loss of income, in addition to medical bills. I explain the definition of lost income and answer common questions about lost wages related to accident claims as we continue to explore personal injury claims and car accidents.

CHAPTER FIVE
Lost Wages

The damages caused by a motor vehicle accident go far beyond physical injuries and emotional suffering. In many traffic accident cases, victims sustain substantial financial losses because of the accident, including loss of income. The loss of income can cause serious financial problems for victims who are struggling to recover from car accident injuries.

I will discuss loss of income after a car accident and how you can recover compensation in more detail.

Loss of Income After an Accident

Even a minor injury caused by a car accident may result in lost time from work. The soreness caused by the collision may require a few days at home using ice packs and over-the-counter medication to recover.

A mild traumatic brain injury (concussion), or whiplash may take a couple of weeks of recovery after a car crash. For some people, a concussion or whiplash can worsen, causing severe complications that could require months or years of therapy and treatments.

Accident victims who sustain catastrophic injuries may face a lifetime of loss of income because of a disability or impairment. Examples of catastrophic injuries include traumatic brain injury, spinal cord injuries, amputations, severe burns, back injuries, neck injuries, and paralysis.

Notwithstanding the injury, an accident victim who loses income because of the negligence of another party is entitled to compensation for financial losses. However, wages are not the only "income" included in a personal injury claim.

Types of Loss of Income

Wages and salaries are the most common types of income included in an accident claim. However, any form of income or benefit may potentially be included as a compensable damage in a car accident claim.

Typical benefits and income in a personal injury claim include, but are not limited to:

Employment Income

Employment income is the financial compensation you receive for providing services as directed by your employer. In addition to wages and salaries, other forms of compensation include bonuses, overtime, and commissions. Any financial payment from your employer intended to compensate you for your work may be included in a loss of income claim.

Self-Employment Income

Independent contractors and business owners may also file a claim for loss of income after a car accident. Independent contractors, or 1099 employees may work for several employers. Each account may represent a loss of income. Business owners may experience a loss of income if they draw a salary. However, they may also experience a loss of income if their profits decrease because they are unable to give 100 percent of their effort to operating their business because of their injuries.

It can be more challenging to calculate the loss of income for a business owner or an independent contractor. I often consult financial experts, accountants, and business experts to analyze the financial records to calculate the loss of income accurately to maximize the amount of money my clients may receive for a loss of income claim.

Benefits

The value of employment benefits is often overlooked when calculating the value of a loss of income claim.

For example, many workers earn PTO (paid time off) and other benefits and perks for each week they work. If you are unable to work, you may not earn PTO time and other benefits. Being unable to earn these benefits because you are unable to work after an accident is a financial loss. Depending on your income level and employment contract, 40 hours of PTO may equal thousands of dollars.

Perks are another loss of benefits that may be included in a personal injury claim. Perks such as stock options, health insurance, transportation allowances, profit-sharing plans, and life insurance are valuable. If you can prove that you lost these perks and the value of these perks, you may be able to recover additional compensation for your injury claim.

Likewise, contributions to your retirement account and matching employer contributions to your retirement account are also benefits that are lost when you are out of work. Missed payroll contributions to Social Security are also a valuable benefit that may be included in a loss of income claim.

Lost Opportunities

When you are out of work because of an accident injury, you can also miss valuable opportunities that has the potential to improve your career or open new opportunities. It can be challenging to determine the value of lost opportunities when you are out of work because of an accident. However, if you have substantial proof that your accident injuries resulted in a lost business opportunity, experts may be helpful in valuing the loss to include the amount when you file your personal injury claim.

Future Loss of Income and Loss of Earning Potential

This type of income loss occurs when your accident injury results in permanent impairment or disability. If you are unable to work, future loss of income would equal the amount of money you would have earned had you not been injured.

The amount of your future loss of income depends on several factors. It is generally necessary to retain one or more experts to value future loss of income correctly.

If your injury results in total disability, a thorough analysis of how much money you may have earned had you kept working depends on factors such as:

- Your age at the time of the accident
- Anticipated life expectancy
- Occupation
- Work and earnings history
- Education
- Experience and skill level
- Economic outlook for your specific industry
- If you can work, but your injury diminishes your earning capacity, additional factors may also be used when calculating future loss of income. Additional factors used when valuing a claim for diminished earning capacity include the type of injury, the severity of the injury, and your ability to compete in the labor market.

Duty to Mitigate Damages

You have a duty to mitigate damages. For example, if you did not complete physical therapy, or did not follow your doctor's treatment plan, the defendant may argue that your actions contributed to the severity of your injury. If your physician testifies that there is a strong possibility that your actions or inactions hindered your recovery, the value of your loss of income claim may be lowered.

The duty to mitigate damages also extends to your job search. If you fail to take reasonable steps to obtain employment, it may hurt your claim. For example, if you do not participate in vocational therapy or occupational therapy prescribed by your physician, the defendant may claim you intentionally reduced the chance of finding new employment.

Filing a Claim to Recover Lost Income After an Accident

If another person is responsible for causing the accident, you will likely file a claim with the insurance company against the at-fault driver. The insurance company will not reimburse you for your loss of income until the claim is settled. Unfortunately, you are responsible for your financial needs while you are recovering from an accident injury. For many people without disability insurance, being injured in an accident can cause severe financial hardship.

Some of the ways that you can help cover expenses while you are recovering from an injury include:

- Using paid vacation time and sick leave from your employer
- Filing a short-term disability claim through an employer-sponsored policy or a private policy that you may have purchased. (Note: If you do file for short-term disability, and recover a settlement from the at-fault party, you may have to repay those short-term disability benefits to the provider.)
- File a claim against coverage that you may have through your car insurance provider, such as Personal Injury Protection (PIP) coverage. Some no-fault insurance policies cover some of your lost wages while you are recovering from your accident
- Use of money you have put into an emergency savings account
- Ask friends or family members for assistance
- Talk to your lenders and creditors. Explain that you are recovering from an accident and ask if there is any assistance that they may provide regarding your bills
- Contact your local government or state agencies to inquire about assistance programs.

Unfortunately, an insurance company knows that you need money. The insurance adjuster may take advantage of the fact that you need money to pay your bills by offering a quick, low settlement offer for your injury claim. The insurance company hopes that you will immediately need the cash and that you will agree to the insurance settlement, saving the insurance company money in the long-term.

If you agree to settle your insurance claim before you complete treatment, you cannot receive any additional money for your injury claim. Therefore, any future medical bills, loss of income, or other damages are your responsibility after you settle the injury claim. Even if you discover a new injury or require additional surgery, you cannot go back to the insurance company or the at-fault driver for more money.

Therefore, it is going to be difficult, but you need to wait until you complete treatment before you settle an injury claim. During that time, there are things you can do to increase the chance that you will recover maximum compensation for your loss of income.

Tips for Improving Chances of Recovering Full Compensation for Loss of Income

As you are recovering from an accident injury, there are things you can do to improve your chances of recovering full compensation for all loss of income and benefits.

1. **Complete your treatment plan.**

As discussed above, you have a duty to mitigate damages. If you do not complete your treatment plan, do not attend follow up appointments with the doctor, or try to return to work before your doctor releases you, you could hurt your chance of recovering full compensation for an injury claim.

2. **Keep a log of all missed time from work.**

Keep a daily log that details all missed time from work. If your job entails overtime during specific periods, make sure to note which days or weeks you would have likely earned overtime based on prior years.

3. **Gather documents.**

You need proof of your past income. Therefore, begin gathering copies of your tax returns, pay stubs, W-2 statements, 1099 statements, and other evidence of your income. You may also request a Wage Verification Statement from your employer to verify your job title, job description, income, and benefits.

Self-employed individuals may also need copies of their business records, such as accounts receivable, balance sheets, and business bank records.

4. **Medical evaluation.**

In addition to evidence proving your loss of income, you need a medical evaluation from your doctor. The medical evaluation needs to state that the accident caused your injuries. The statement must also describe the type and extent of your injuries, how your injuries prevented you from working, and the type and extent of any permanent impairment. You cannot recover compensation unless you can prove that your injuries resulted from the automobile accident, and you were unable to work because of your injuries.

5. **Proof of fault for the accident.**

You cannot recover compensation from the other driver unless you prove that the other driver caused the car accident. A personal injury lawyer can conduct a thorough accident investigation to determine how the accident occurred and who is responsible for the cause of the accident. The attorney gathers evidence to prove fault so that you can hold the at-fault driver liable for your loss of income and other damages.

6. **Hire medical and financial experts.**

Depending on the complexity of your injury case, you may need medical experts to help you prove that your injuries resulted from the crash. You must also prove your loss of income and benefits that were caused by the crash. Financial experts and economists calculate the loss based on the factors we discussed above. A medical expert provides additional information for the financial experts to use as part of their basis for calculating the future loss of income and benefits based on your prognosis and impairment rating.

7. **Hire an experienced personal injury lawyer as soon as possible.**

Loss of income damages in an accident case can be one of the more challenging aspects of calculating the value of an injury claim. The value of the loss of income claim relies heavily on other aspects of the case, including proving fault and obtaining medical evidence. Documenting loss of income can also be complicated, especially if you are unable to assist in gathering information because of your injury.

Having an experienced lawyer on your side can give you a better chance of recovering full compensation for your injuries. An injury lawyer understands how to gather evidence, prove fault, and calculate damages. An attorney understands the tactics used by insurance companies to deny and undervalue valid injury claims. The insurance company has a team working to protect its best interest. You need and deserve a team of professionals protecting your best interests while you recover from accident injuries.

IMPORTANT NOTE: Some states have short deadlines to file personal injury lawsuits. If a government entity or agency is involved in the claim, you could have as little as a few months to file a notice of claim to protect your right to compensation for injuries, losses, and damages.

It is a wise idea to talk to a personal injury lawyer as soon as possible, even if you have not completed medical treatment. You may need to take steps to protect your legal rights to ensure your time to file a personal injury lawsuit does not expire before you are ready to make a claim.

Commonly Asked Questions About Recovering Loss of Income After an Accident

If I was scheduled to take a vacation right after I was injured, am I entitled to be paid lost wages for that time?

Even though you may have been scheduled for a vacation before the accident, you may have changed your mind about taking the time off. If you were unable to work because of your injury, you are entitled to compensation for loss of income.

However, if you use vacation time to pay for those missed days of work, you are not be entitled to compensation for loss of income. You are entitled to the loss of your vacation time. You were forced to use your vacation time, which is a benefit provided by your company, to cover your wages while you were out of work because of an injury that was not your fault. Therefore, you lost that benefit because of the accident and may be reimbursed for the loss of vacation time.

You cannot "double-dip" when claiming loss of income. In other words, you cannot claim that you are entitled to compensation for loss of wages if you used your vacation time as compensation for missing work because of the accident. You are compensated for either the actual loss of income, or the loss of vacation time.

However, you can include a claim for loss of benefits if you lose future PTO (paid time off) because you are unable to work. For example, you earn one hour of PTO for each week you work. If you are out of work for 12 weeks because of the injury, you lost 12 hours of PTO, which can be included as a loss in your personal injury claim.

I was out of work at the time of the accident, but I was looking for work. I was unable look for work after the accident because of my injuries. How can I get compensated for that time?

You may receive compensation for a loss of opportunity or loss of potential earnings. If your injuries prevent you from continuing to actively look for a job while you recover from an accident, you may receive compensation for missing interviews and losing job opportunities. It is similar to an independent contractor or someone who receives commissions. The person may not have had an open job at the time of the accident, but the accident now prevents the person from actively seeking new opportunities to earn money.

You will need medical evidence proving that you are unable to work because of your injuries. It will also help to have evidence that you were actively seeking employment when the accident occurred.

I got fired from my job because I could not go back to work after the accident. Does the insurance company have to pay for me losing my job?

You may be entitled to compensation for wages that you may have earned for your period of disability, but it is unlikely that you will be compensated for losing your job. You are only compensated for the injuries that you have sustained as a result of the accident.

Additionally, depending on the state in which you reside and the circumstances of the firing, you may potentially have a wrongful termination lawsuit against your employer. It is best to consult an experienced personal injury lawyer as soon as possible in this situation. There may be several courses of action available for compensation.

I can no longer do the type of work that I did before the accident, is the insurance company responsible for those damages?

This type of damage would fall under a **loss of earning capacity**. When a person sustains an injury that results in a permanent impairment, that person may be entitled to compensation for loss of earning potential. The value of the claim is the difference between the amount of money you would have earned but for the injury, and the amount of money you are expected to earn now given your impairment.

For example, assume the victim was a Registered Nurse earning $80,000 yearly before the accident. Because of her injuries, the nurse cannot remain on her feet for more than a few hours a day. This impairment severely limits the types of positions she may qualify for in the future. If the maximum amount she might earn in the future is $40,000 yearly, her loss of earning potential would be $40,000 per year.

Loss of earning potential cases are very complex. Medical and financial experts are required to help prove that the injury will result in a substantial loss of income over the person's lifetime.

Is compensation for loss of income in a personal injury claim taxable income?

In most cases, the compensation received for a personal injury claim is non-taxable provided that your claim involves a physical injury. However, there are exceptions. It is always best to discuss this matter with an experienced personal injury lawyer, and your tax professional before agreeing to a settlement. The exceptions are specific and do not apply to most people, but it is best to know the answer before you agree to a settlement agreement.

Settling Your Personal Injury Claim

So far, I have discussed what you should do if you are injured in an accident, and damages that are compensable in an injury claim. While most personal injury claims settle out of court, some cases proceed to trial.

In the next chapter, I discuss the requirement for an insurance company to investigate an accident claim. I also cover what happens if your case goes to trial, such as preparing for trial and what to expect at trial.

CHAPTER SIX

Trial Tips

Most personal injury claims are settled without a lawsuit being filed. Some claims are settled after a personal injury lawsuit is filed but before the case goes to trial. However, there are cases for which a trial is necessary to settle disputed issues so that each party can have a resolution to the matter.

Requirement to Investigate Insurance Claims

Insurance companies are required to investigate a personal injury claim. Failing to take reasonable steps to investigate an insurance claim may give an injured party cause to file a bad faith insurance lawsuit. Therefore, insurance companies have at least two reasons to investigate an insurance claim thoroughly.

The first reason is to avoid allegations of bad faith insurance tactics. The second reason is to try to limit liability for the claim. Insurance companies strive to pay as little as possible to settle or resolve an injury claim. Uncovering evidence that supports its desire to deny or undervalue a claim is a strong incentive to investigate personal injury claims thoroughly and aggressively.

Depending on the facts of the case, it can take an insurance company weeks or months to investigate a claim.

Why Do Some Accident Investigations Take Longer to Complete?

Each case is unique. The causes of some accidents are easy to determine. For example, a driver turns left at a red light in front of oncoming traffic and causes a collision. There are witnesses who verify that the driver turning left did not have the right-of-way. A traffic camera also catches the collision, thereby supporting the accident victim's claim that the other driver caused the crash.

Unfortunately, not all accident cases are easy to investigate. Certain factors can complicate an accident investigation.

For example, large truck accident claims can take over a year to investigate. In addition to the typical issues involved when investigating the cause of a traffic accident, the insurance company must also carefully review the evidence to determine if the truck driver or the trucking company violated federal laws and regulations that govern the operation of commercial vehicles. Furthermore, the information on the truck's black box could take months to analyze. Experts may be hired to examine the truck carefully for malfunctions or defective parts.

Multi-vehicle accidents can also take longer to investigate. The multiple insurance companies involved in the case have an incentive to gather as much evidence as possible proving their insured was not responsible for the crash, or that other drivers had a higher degree of fault for the cause of the accident.

Accidents that involves only two vehicles can be complicated to investigate if both drivers deny fault, and there are no witnesses or video evidence to determine which driver is telling the truth. In these cases, the insurance company may need to retain experts and an accident reconstructionist to try to prove its driver was not responsible for causing the crash.

Even though the insurance company may complete an investigation quickly, that does not mean that your injury claim will settle quickly. The accident investigation is only one factor in how long it takes to settle a personal injury claim. Two additional factors are the victim's length of recovery, and the insurance company's acceptance of liability after its investigation.

It is Unwise to Settle an Injury Claim before Your Doctors Release You from Care

Another factor in the time-line for settling a personal injury claim is your recovery from injuries. An insurance company may pressure you to settle your claim before your doctor releases you from treatment. The company may offer a quick settlement because it has already completed the investigation and understands that its insured driver is responsible for causing the crash. By immediately settling the claim, the company hopes to lower the amount it must pay to settle your claim.

However, if you settle your claim before you complete treatment, you could lose thousands of dollars in compensation. When you accept a settlement from the insurance company, that amount is the total amount of money you receive for your claim. You are required to sign an agreement releasing the insurance company, the driver, and all parties involved in the accident from further liability for your damages.

If you are still receiving treatment for your injuries, you may incur additional expenses. The insurance company may agree to increase the settlement amount slightly to cover the anticipated cost of treatment.

However, there is no way to know for sure if the settlement covers all future medical care and losses. For example, if your doctor discovers an additional injury, or advises you that you need surgery or other treatment, you cannot receive additional compensation for the additional costs if you have already settled your claim with the insurance company. You are limited to the settlement you received.

Furthermore, if you discover that you have a disability or permanent impairment, you cannot go back to the insurance company for more money. If you are unable to work for the rest of your life, or you are limited in the amount of money you earn, you are not entitled to additional compensation after you settle the claim.

Therefore, you should wait to settle your claim until you complete medical treatment, and your doctor has determined if you have sustained a permanent impairment or disability. You want to ensure that you include future damages and losses in the amount of your personal injury claim.

The bottom line is that you cannot know the full value of your injury claim until you complete treatment. Settling an injury claim too early may result in receiving a much lower amount of compensation than you would have received had you waited until you completed treatment to settle your claim.

Insurance Companies Always Estimate the Value of a Personal Injury Claim

Your case may not be worth as much as you think your case is worth. Injury claims are only worth as much as a jury would award for the case. Insurance companies are aware of this fact when they are investigating the claim and negotiating a settlement for your claim. Therefore, if the insurance company believes that it can make a convincing argument during a trial to avoid liability, the insurance company may refuse to pay the value of the claim that you believe to be just and fair.

There are numerous reasons why an insurance company may believe it has a better chance of getting out of paying a claim or paying less to settle a claim by going to trial. These include:

- There is evidence it believes supports its arguments that its insured driver did not cause the crash
- The insurance company believes it can prove your injuries are not as severe as you claim
- There is evidence that you may share responsibility for causing the accident
- The insurance company believes that it can prove the accident did not cause your injuries
- The company has analyzed jury awards in your jurisdiction and believes it can limit liability by taking the case to trial.

For the insurance company, it is a matter of weighing all factors during a risk assessment to determine which option is in the company's best interest.

Your personal injury lawyer also analyzes all factors before advising you if you should accept a settlement or proceed to trial. Going to trial is never a guarantee that you will receive a substantial award for your claim.

In some cases, accident victims may not receive as much by going to trial. The expense and time involved in a trial may cost more than the additional compensation a person may expect to receive by going to trial. Also, juries are unpredictable. Even though the evidence appears to be in favor of one party, a jury could return a verdict based on emotion. The jury hears the evidence presented in court, but the jury may choose which evidence it uses when deciding the case.

Insurance companies understand the unpredictability of jury trials. They consider this factor when deciding whether to accept a settlement offer from an injury victim. Personal injury lawyers who have trial experience also understand this factor. Your personal injury attorney advises you based on all factors in your case. It is your decision whether you move forward with a lawsuit or agree to accept the settlement the insurance company agrees to pay.

What Can You Do To Prepare for a Potential Personal Injury Lawsuit?

Even though many injury claims settle without the need to file a personal injury lawsuit, it is a good idea to treat your case as if you are preparing for a trial. The things you do during your recovery can have a significant impact on the outcome of a trial. Even if your case settles before trial, the following four tips can help you increase your chance of recovering maximum compensation when you settle your personal injury claim.

1. Follow Your Medical Treatment Plan Until Your Doctor Releases You

Prompt medical treatment is crucial in personal injury cases. You need medical evidence documenting your injuries. The medical evidence also helps link your injuries to the accident, which is essential for receiving compensation from the person who caused the accident.

Accident victims who do not receive medical treatment may be accused of failing to mitigate the damages caused by the accident. In other words, you made your injuries worse than they were because you did not seek medical care, delayed medical treatment, or failed to complete your medical treatment.

Going to the doctor once or twice is not sufficient. You must follow your doctor's treatment plan until your doctor releases you. Your treatment plan may require you to stay out of work for a certain period, complete physical therapy, or have surgery. If you disagree with the treatment plan, seek a second opinion, but be careful. Delays in medical care may hurt your case. The insurance company may argue that your injuries were not sustained in the accident. Try to find a doctor you trust as soon as possible and work with that doctor to develop a treatment plan that gives you the best chance of a full recovery.

2. **Start an Accident Journal**

An Accident Journal may also be referred to as a Pain and Suffering Journal or Recovery Journal. The purpose of an accident journal is to keep notes about your recovery in case you need to testify in court. It can be challenging to remember the details of how you suffered after your accident without notes. It can also be helpful to provide details your attorney can include in a settlement demand.

The journal contains details about your injury and your recovery, such as your daily pain levels, activities that you can not perform because of your injuries, and events you missed because you were injured. You may also include details about how your injuries impacted your relationship with family members and friends. For instance, you and your partner were unable to engage in intimate activities; you were unable to coach your son's baseball team as you have for the last several years; or, you missed a crucial business conference that would have significantly improved your career choices.

You may also include notes about your emotional state during recovery. For example, did you have nightmares or flashbacks of the accident? Did you become depressed or have severe anxiety about riding in a vehicle after the accident? Any detail, regardless of how unimportant it may seem, may be the detail that helps your attorney prove the extent of your damages after an accident.

3. **Document Financial Losses**

Your personal injury lawyer assists you in gathering proof of financial losses. The attorney typically requests a statement of fees and costs from each medical provider. The attorney may also request a statement from your employer regarding the loss of income.

However, there may be financial losses that your attorney may not be aware of without your help. Financial losses and expenses that you need to document for your attorney include, but may not be limited to:

- Travel expenses, including mileage to and from doctor's visits and medical treatments
- Expenses related to over-the-counter medications and medical supplies
- Payment for help with house cleaning, mowing the yard, and other household chores you cannot perform
- Expenses related to personal care, such as someone to help you bathe or dress
- Loss of income your spouse may experience to care for you or take you to appointments
- Modifications to your home to accommodate any impairments caused by the injuries

Keep copies of invoices, receipts, and other proof of the expenses and your payment of the expenses.

4. **Avoid Using Social Media Accounts**

If your case goes to trial, a defense attorney may obtain copies of your social media posts or other information. In some cases, courts have granted access to an accident victim's social media accounts and other information that the person may have thought was private. It is wise to remember that anything you post online is never really private.

As I discussed earlier in this chapter, a jury is unpredictable. A defense attorney could spin a convincing story arguing that you cannot be injured if you went bowling at your niece's birthday party, went on vacation, or went swimming at your in-law's house. It does not matter that you were in severe pain and did nothing but sit and watch others have fun. If there are pictures of you attending the events, a jury may believe what the defense attorney says.

Do not give the defense attorney any additional information that he can use against you. It is best to stop using social media accounts after an accident until your claim is settled or your case is heard by a jury, including posting on blogs or in chat rooms.

What Can You Expect if You File a Personal Injury Lawsuit?

Each personal injury lawsuit is unique. You cannot base your lawsuit or the outcome of your lawsuit on any previous lawsuit. State laws vary regarding injury lawsuits. Additionally, courts may have slightly different rules and procedures for how they handle lawsuits. However, certain steps take place in almost all personal injury lawsuits.

Filing a Personal Injury Lawsuit

The case begins by filing a complaint. The complaint outlines the facts of the case and the allegations against the other party. The party who files the complaint is the plaintiff. The party the complaint is filed against is the defendant. There can be more than one defendant in the case.

In your complaint, you must set forth facts that show that the defendant was negligent. This means you must show that the defendant had a duty to operate their vehicle in a safe manner.

There are four elements you must show to prove negligence:

1. Duty
2. Breach
3. Causation
4. Damages

If you fail to include facts about each of these elements, your lawsuit will fail. You must therefore show that the defendant breached that duty, and that because of that breach of duty, you were damaged.

Answers and Counterclaims

The defendants have a certain number of days to respond to the complaint. In most states, defendants have 30 days from the date they are served with the complaint.

The response is called an answer. The answer responds to the allegations contained in the complaint. The answer may admit factual information, such as the date of the accident and the parties involved, and deny the remaining allegations regarding fault.

The defendant may also file a counterclaim. A counterclaim sets forth allegations against the plaintiff. The defendant claims that the plaintiff was negligent or guilty of wrongdoing and should compensate the defendant for losses and damages. If a defendant files a counterclaim, the plaintiff can file a response to the counterclaim.

Discovery Phase

The discovery phase allows each party to request information and evidence from the other party. The intent is to share information that will be used in court as evidence. The discovery phase allows the parties to learn more about the other side's case. It also is a chance to uncover new evidence that may support a party's allegations.

Examples of tools used during the discovery phase include:

- Interrogatories – Questions a party must answer under oath
- Requests for Admission – Statements a party must admit or deny under oath
- Request to Produce – List of documents the other side requests from a party
- Depositions – Questions asked under oath. The answers have the same weight as testimony in court. However, the rules of testimony in court do not apply in depositions. Depositions are used to take testimony from a party to the case, witnesses, or experts.

Motions

There are several different types of motions that may be filed before the trial. These motions may relate to the admissibility of evidence or whether a witness may testify about certain information. Motions may also be used to compel parties to provide the information requested during discovery. The defendant may file a motion to dismiss the case. Some motions are made at the beginning of a trial. Some motions are made at the end of the trial before the jury arrives at a verdict.

Mediation

Some states require parties to an auto accident to go through mandatory mediation. In other states, mediation is a type of alternative dispute resolution that is much less formal than a typical trial. Mediations are less expensive than trials and are resolved quicker than trials. Instead of a judge, the case is decided by a third-party dispute resolution specialist—sometimes called a "neutral" because they are a neutral third party. This person is typically a retired judge or attorney experienced in personal injury cases.

In a mediation, both parties file a mediation brief with the mediator, along with the evidence to support their claims. The parties meet face-to-face in the mediation, represented by their attorneys. The mediator will ask questions of both parties. There is no jury. Often, the mediator will separate the parties and ask further questions in an attempt to get the parties to come to an agreement.

If the parties come to an agreement, the mediator will draft a mediation agreement that binds all of the parties. If the parties cannot reach an agreement, the case goes to trial.

Trial

The trial allows each party to present its case to the jury. The plaintiff goes first, followed by the defendant. Each side may present witnesses to offer testimony and admit evidence into the record. Testimony and evidence at a trial are governed by very specific rules and laws, which can be frustrating if you are not allowed to present certain evidence you feel is vital to the case.

At the end of the trial, the jury deliberates. A jury must come to a unanimous decision in personal injury cases. If the jury cannot arrive at a unanimous decision, the judge may grant a mistrial. The plaintiff may request a new trial.

Appeals

If either party does not agree with the jury's verdict, that party may appeal to a higher court. For that reason, a jury verdict does not guarantee payment of a claim. If the jury finds in your favor and awards you a specific amount for damages, you may not receive that amount for a long time. If the defendant appeals the case, it could take years for the case to work its way through the entire appeals process. Your case could be overturned on appeal.

Because there are no guarantees in a trial, accepting a settlement offer may be the best chance you have of receiving a fair amount for your personal injury claim. However, you may need to file a lawsuit if the insurance company refuses to negotiate in good faith. The best way to protect your legal rights is to talk to an experienced injury lawyer. A lawyer analyzes your case, reviews the relevant factors, and researches the laws and case results to provide advice about your options and what may be best in your case.

In the final chapter, I review the information provided in this book and provide additional tips and suggestions you can use if you have been injured in an accident.

CHAPTER SEVEN
Conclusion

As I discussed in the Foreword, my purpose in creating this book is to help accident victims understand what happens after an accident, and what they can expect as they go through the process of filing a personal injury claim. I hope that the information in this book has helped you understand the claims process. I also hope that you have found the information helpful as you begin the process of seeking compensation from the party who caused your injuries.

Let's review some of the key elements discussed in each chapter.

Chapter One – The First Steps

In Chapter One, I discussed some of the steps that you should take if you are involved in a car accident. I also discussed what you could expect in the weeks following an accident.

The steps you take after a car accident can help or hurt your chance of recovering full compensation for a car accident claim. Because the moments after a car crash can result in confusion and shock, it is worth repeating those steps again in a short **checklist** that you can print and keep in your vehicle.

Steps to Take at the scene of a Motor Vehicle Accident

Check for injuries. Check yourself and then check others involved in the accident.

Access the accident scene for danger. If you can move your vehicle out of traffic, do so. If you smell gasoline or you are in immediate danger, move to a safe location.

Call 911 to report the accident and request emergency services.

Avoid discussing the accident with other drivers or passengers.

Never apologize, say you are sorry, or otherwise admit fault for contributing to the cause of the accident.

Take pictures and a video of the accident scene. Never place yourself or others in danger. Capture as much of the accident scene and the vehicles as possible.

Take notes about statements other people make at the accident scene, including other drivers, passengers, and witnesses. If you do not have a pen or paper, text yourself notes or use your cell phone to record notes.

Ask witnesses for their names and contact information.

Seek medical attention as soon as possible. Do not say that you are not injured. If you are unsure about your injuries, it is okay to tell a police officer you intend to be checked by your doctor as soon as possible.

Go to the emergency room if you are in pain or believe your injuries may be severe.

Always make a police report. If police officers do not respond to the accident for any reason, contact your local police department to file a police report as soon as possible.

Steps to Take In the Weeks After a Car Accident

Continue with your medical treatment plan. Make sure you attend all doctor appointments and comply with your doctor's orders.

Start a health journal to track your daily pain level, symptoms, treatments, and other information related to your recovery. Include information about activities you cannot perform and how your injuries impact your daily life and relationships with family and friends.

Set up file folders to keep copies of important documents, such as medical bills, receipts, mileage, bills, and other documents that prove damages. Damages include financial losses, physical pain, and emotional suffering.

Contact your insurance company to report the accident. You may have insurance coverage that can help with some of the medical bills and other expenses related to the accident.

Avoid speaking to insurance adjusters and claims adjusters. The insurance company for the other driver is not on your side. It wants to pay as little as possible for your claim. Therefore, it is best not to talk to anyone who is representing the other insurance provider.

Contact a personal injury lawyer for help. An attorney can give you additional guidance on steps to take and mistakes to avoid. Your lawyer works to protect your best interests and get you as much money as possible for your claim.

Chapter Two – Insurance Coverage

In Chapter Two, I discussed the various insurance coverages that may apply in a car accident claim. Briefly, the insurance coverages I discussed were:

- **Collision Coverage** — Pays for damage to your vehicle when it collides with another vehicle or object. Collision coverage applies in cases in which the accident was your fault. Most lenders require collision coverage to protect their loans.
- **Comprehensive Coverage** — Pays for damage to your vehicle from other covered events unrelated to car accidents, such as fire, theft, vandalism, and storm damage. Lenders also require comprehensive coverage to protect their loans.
- **Liability Coverage** — Liability insurance coverage pays compensation for damages sustained by accident victims when you cause a car accident.
- **Uninsured Motorist Coverage** — UM coverage helps pay you compensation if you are injured in an accident caused by an uninsured driver.
- **Underinsured Motorist Coverage** — UIM coverage can provide additional compensation to you if an at-fault driver's

liability insurance does not pay your claim in full.

- **Underinsured Motorist Coverage —** UMC will be applied to a case when an at-fault driver does not have sufficient coverage to handle the damage that he/she has caused. Once you have exhausted the policy limits of the at-fault carrier, you make a claim with your own company so they can pay you the remaining amount owed.
- **Umbrella Coverage** — Umbrella insurance covers damages and losses that exceed the typical insurance coverage. You should carefully read the coverages for an umbrella policy to ensure you are receiving the coverage you desire.
- **Personal Injury Protection or Medical Payments Coverage** — PIP or Med-Pay insurance is a form of no-fault car insurance. No-fault insurance pays for covered losses, regardless of which driver caused the accident. Depending on the policy, PIP insurance may also reimburse you for some of your lost wages after a car crash.

Car insurance is an important financial tool that everyone needs to protect themselves and others in the event of an accident or other disaster. It is generally recommended that drivers carry the highest levels of insurance coverage they can afford to protect themselves and their assets and property.

I concluded the chapter by answering some of the most common insurance questions I receive from clients.

Chapter Three – Recovery and Healing

The recovery and healing process is different for everyone. The type and severity of injuries are the main factors that impact the length of recovery after a car accident. However, overall health and pre-existing conditions and injuries may also impact recovery time.

Three of the most important issues that I covered in Chapter Three were:

1. **Do not Delay Medical Treatment**

Delays in medical care can hurt your chance of recovering fair compensation for your injury claim. Insurance companies search for any reason to undervalue car accident claims. If you do not receive medical care soon after your car accident, the insurance company may claim that the accident was not the cause of your injuries. The company may argue that if you were injured in the accident, you would have sought medical treatment sooner. Because you waited to seek medical treatment, your injuries must have occurred after the car accident.

It is generally best to be checked by a doctor within a few days following a car accident. The only way you can know for sure whether you were injured in a car accident is to be checked by a medical provider.

2. Complete Medical Treatment

Insurance companies often offer quick, low settlements to injury victims before the individuals understand the full extent of their injuries. The settlement offers are a way for the insurance company to save money. The claim may be worth much more once the person completes medical treatment.

However, once you settle your car accident claim, you cannot go back to the insurance company for more money.

It is best to wait until you reach maximum medical improvement (MMI). MMI is the point at which you have recovered as much as possible with medical treatment. At this point, your doctor will provide a statement assigning an impairment rating and describing any impairments or disabilities caused by accident injuries.

3. Types of Damages in a Car Accident Claims

The types of damages sustained in a car accident fall into two general categories, economic and noneconomic damages.

Economic damages include, but are not limited to:

- Medical expenses and bills
- Personal care expenses
- Loss of income
- Travel expenses

- Help with household chores
- Out-of-pocket expenses

Noneconomic damages (pain and suffering damages) included, but are not limited to:

- Physical suffering and pain
- Emotional distress, including PTSD, anxiety, and depression
- Mental anguish
- Loss of enjoyment of life
- Decrease in quality of life
- Scarring, disability, impairments, and disfigurement
- Punitive damages (rare in car accident claims)

There is not a standard equation for valuing noneconomic damages. The value of your claim depends on many factors, including the type of injuries, the severity of injuries, and total financial losses.

Carefully documenting all damages can increase the chance you receive maximum value for your injury claim., An experienced injury lawyer understands how to value car accident claims and maximize the value of noneconomic damages.

Chapter Four – Medical Bills

Chapter Four discussed the common medical treatments that many people need after a car accident. Depending on your injuries, you may require surgery, hospitalization, various forms of therapy, personal care, and special medical equipment. In cases involving permanent disabilities, you may need ongoing medical care and personal care.

The cost of medical care after a car accident can be extremely expensive. Health insurance may be used to pay for treatment, but remember, the health insurance company will expect reimbursement of payments when you receive compensation from the other driver. The right to be reimbursed for health insurance payments related to the car accident is a subrogation claim.

Med Pay and PIP coverage can also help pay medical bills after a car accident. However, you may not have enough coverage to pay all medical bills. If you cannot pay your medical bills, some providers may continue treatment if you sign an agreement promising to pay the medical bills from your settlement proceeds before you receive any money.

Your attorney may be able to negotiate with medical providers and your health insurance company to lower the amount you must pay to satisfy medical liens and subrogation claims. Your attorney may also be able to negotiate with medical providers who have not been paid to lower the amount you must pay to satisfy the debt, especially if your settlement proceeds do not cover all damages and losses caused by the car accident.

Chapter Five — Lost Wages

Chapter Five discusses lost wages. Loss of income and medical expenses are two of the largest financial losses incurred by a car accident victim. In this chapter, I discussed the types of loss of income that a person may experience after a car accident. I also answered some common questions regarding loss of income claims.

The loss of income is not limited to wages and salaries. A loss of income may also include loss of income from self-employment. It also includes the loss of opportunities and loss of benefits.

If you are unable to work because of a disability or you cannot earn the same income level you did before the accident because of your injury, you may also be entitled to future loss of income. Future loss of income can total millions of dollars for accident victims who are completely disabled after an accident.

To recover compensation, you must have evidence to support your claim. Expert testimony is essential in these cases.

Chapter Six — Trial Tips

Most car accident claims settle without filing a personal injury lawsuit. In most cases, it is less costly and faster to settle an injury claim without filing a lawsuit. Unfortunately, insurance companies want to pay as little as possible to settle your claim. The insurance company investigates the accident to determine fault. In cases of clear fault, the insurance company may decide it is less costly to pay your claim and end the case.

However, if the insurance company believes that it may have one or more defenses that it can use to argue its driver did not cause the accident, the insurance company may take its chances in court. Your personal injury lawyer weighs all options and advises you whether it is better to accept the company's settlement offer or proceed to trial.

If you contributed to the cause of the car accident, you might want to accept the settlement offer. All states have contributory fault or comparative negligence laws that allow the court to reduce your compensation by the percentage of fault assigned to you. Therefore, if there is strong evidence proving you contributed to the cause of the car crash, taking a settlement offer might be in your best interest.

In cases in which an insurance company is acting in bad faith or merely refusing to pay a fair amount to settle your claim, you may need to proceed with a personal injury lawsuit. Some of the steps in a lawsuit that I discussed in Chapter Six included:

- Fining the complaint alleging fault and liability against the defendant and other parties
- The defendant responds by filing an answer and possibly a counterclaim
- The discovery phase allows both parties to use several tools to collect information from the other party and additional evidence
- Parties may file several motions before trial
- The trial gives all parties the chance to present their case to the jury
- The jury returns a verdict for one party
- Either party may file an appeal if the party does not agree with the verdict.

Preparing for trial can seem overwhelming. However, your personal injury attorney gives you advice and guidance. Your attorney may advise you to begin an accident journal, if you have not started one already. Your accident journal can help document your suffering throughout your recovery.

Staying Safe On The Road

Distracted drivers, intoxicated drivers, and reckless drivers cause millions of car accidents each year. Their actions can change the lives of innocent accident victims forever.

Some tips that can help you stay safe when you are on the road include:

- Decrease distractions while driving. Do not use cell phones or other electronic devices. Keep your focus on the road.
- Never operate a motor vehicle after consuming alcohol or using drugs.
- Do not drive when you are tired or drowsy.
- Always wear seat belts. If you ride a bicycle or motorcycle, always wear a helmet and protective gear.
- Maintain your vehicle. A vehicle that is adequately maintained is safer. Check for recalls on the NHTSA website or talk to your dealer about potential safety recalls.
- Reduce speed. Driving over the speed limit or driving too fast for conditions can increase the risk of an accident.
- Set a good example for your teen drivers. Always practice safe driving behaviors when kids are in the car.

The National Highway Traffic Safety Administration[2] (NHTSA), the Centers for Disease Control[3], and AAA Exchange[4] provide additional information about staying safe on the road on their websites.

Unfortunately, even the safest drivers can be injured in a car accident that was not their fault. If you are injured in a car crash, remember to take steps to protect your legal rights, including talking to a personal injury lawyer.

---

2 https://one.nhtsa.gov/Driving-Safety
3 https://www.cdc.gov/motorvehiclesafety/index.html
4 https://exchange.aaa.com/safety/

Protecting Your Legal Rights

As I explained in the Foreword to this book, I have represented thousands of clients injured in car accidents during my career. I have witnessed the suffering, pain, emotional distress, and financial hardships caused by reckless drivers and negligent third parties.

My goal in writing this book was to provide you with information and tips regarding car accident claims, from what to do immediately after an accident to steps that you can take to protect your right to fair compensation. I hope that you will never need the information; however, if you are involved in a car accident, I want you to have the information that I did not have as a car accident victim.

Thank you for taking the time to read my book. I hope you found it helpful. If you have additional questions about car accident claims, please don't hesitate to contact me.

Made in United States
Troutdale, OR
11/03/2026

56852693R00049